Poetically Justified

Rascal Dolihan

BookLeaf Publishing

India | USA | UK

Presentation by *BookLeaf Publishing*

Web: www.bookleafpub.com

E-mail: info@bookleafpub.com

ISBN: 978-93-5744-991-5

First edition 2022

DEDICATION

This is for the loves of my life, for letting their light fill the cracks of my heart.

ACKNOWLEDGEMENT

To the friends and family who have encouraged me to write, to the teachers who showed me I could, and to you for reading this, thank you.

PREFACE

I hope this is a wild ride,
I want you to laugh and cry,
I want what I have to write,
To help get you through the night.

I Haven't Always Been

I haven't always been sunflowers.
I have often been the flowers placed,
In sorrow,
At the headstone of the departed.

Less the embodiment of golden hours,
Of warmth and happiness embraced,
And more,
A symbol of mourning and the broken-hearted.

I haven't always been the coffee,
Warming your bones on cold mornings,
I have often been the last dregs of liquor,
Forgotten and gathering dust on the shelf.

You won't always want to wake up to me.
I won't always ease away your bad dreams.
I will often feel like I'm your last resort,
And always like I'm bad for your health.

I haven't always been a clear blue sky.
I have often been the storm clouds,

Gathering tight,
And then pouring out everything inside.

I don't always let the birds inside me fly,
And the things I hold in would astound,
But I'll,
Feel better when I've finally cried.

I haven't always been a holiday gift.
I have often been more like Pandora's box,
A prison,
For all the damage and sins of humanity.

Not a loving thought to make your spirit lift.
But a trick as cunning as a wicked fox.
Opened only,
As an act of morbid and dangerous curiosity.

I haven't always been put together,
I have often been cracked and bruised,
And now,
I'm scared to pick up all the pieces.

Each storm that I couldn't weather,
Has left me beaten up and overused.
But now,
I have you to help until my fear eases.

A Letter to My Abuser

I've grown hair you'll never touch.

I've gotten tattoos you'll never see.

I've washed away the feel of you on my skin.

Nothing in my home smells like you anymore.

I have a new cat you'll never pet.
My other cat would no longer recognize you.

You'll never make me feel crazy again.

You'll never put your foot in a door
I'm trying to close to get space from you,
And claim that I'm the one who hurt you.

You'll never tell me the poem I wrote,
Detailing my most important dreams,
Isn't enough in your eyes.

I don't remember how it feels to kiss you.

I don't remember how it feels to hold your hand.

I don't cry when I see you in town anymore.

Nothing in my dreams reminds me of you.

I have new friends you'll never know.
My old friends would spit in your face.

You'll never make me feel fat again.

You'll never tell me I'm being too loud,
In the home of my mother and father,
When they cannot defend me.

You'll never tell me my gender identity
Is linked to my mental illness,
And then ignore the way it makes me feel.

I hold myself differently because of you.

I hold my lovers further away than I should.

I hold my standards higher than I ever have.

Nothing has ever hurt me like you did.

I have a new job you'll never hear about.
My coworkers there will never know about you.

You'll never get to hear me sing again.

You'll never again see my boundless joy,
Or be the cause of my profound sadness.
And you'll never ignite my burning rage.

You'll never make me question my strength,
Or my very perception of reality.
I know now I can endure the worst.

You'll never get to know who I've become,
In spite of you.

In the Mirror

Yesterday,
I looked in the mirror and saw myself.
I didn't see my mother's child.
I didn't see my lover's partner.
I didn't see my abuser's survivor.

I just saw me.
I looked in the mirror and saw Rascal.
I saw my tattoos and their meaning.
I saw my curves and their softness.
I saw my pink hair and it's vibrancy.

How have I missed this?
I looked in the mirror and saw my pieces.
I'm flowers and art and thighs.
I'm rainbows and pink and yellow.
I'm necklaces and rings and piercings.

Where have I been so long?
I looked in the mirror and saw my repairs.
I saw the gold I poured into myself.
I saw the cracks sealing back up.
I saw the new and whole beauty I am.

To the Person I'll Raise

1. Set your boundaries,
The people you're afraid to lose doing it,
The people that prove you right
Were never meant to stay.

2. Define yourself,
Others will try and do it for you
So start early and remember,
Only you can have a say.

3. Always dream bigger,
When you have the things you wanted,
Find new things to want and start again,
It will help you through each day.

4. Hold your loved ones close,
Someday you will have to let them go,
So grab on to every day with them,
Before those moments go away.

5. Strength isn't physical,
It's more about what you do with pain,

I won't say you'll never have any,
But you choose what to do with it's weight.

6. You are not too much,
The right people will make you feel
As if having you in their lives,
Enriches every single day.

7. You are so beautiful,
This has nothing to do with what's outside,
Beauty lies in your bones and heart,
Never mind how you feel about your face.

8. Always seek comfort,
Whether this is a warm place to go to sleep,
Or someone who helps shoulder your burden,
Be sure to seek out your happy place.

9. You deserve love.
You deserve to be treated as if
You hung the stars and helped the sun rise,
Settling for less is not okay.

10. You can always come home.
If everything else gets to be too much,
There's a place for you in my arms,
That will never be too far away.

The Cloud

Every dark thing I've ever felt or thought,
Lives above me in a stormy cloud,
And I can hear the thunder rumble,
But it's not ready to pour it out.

The air feels almost statically charged,
With the lightning of my every fear.
And everyone has put on raincoats,
But no one is standing with me here.

I know I'm the only one in the dark,
This cloud is all my own darkness and
No one else will even feel it's rain,
But I just wish someone would hold my hand.

The meteorologists don't see my cloud,
They tell me it isn't there or isn't real,
But it blocks so much light from me
Or at least that's how it makes me feel.

It's been so long since I've seen the sun,
It's cold and dim under here alone
And I've been by myself with it for so long,
I don't know when I lost track but it's grown.

Sometimes it feels like someone else sees it,
And they try and make the day brighter.
It's people like that that help me,
And make my heavy cloud feel lighter.

Sometimes someone comes along with a cloud,
All their own thoughts, sadness and fear,
And they know how it feels and see mine.
I hold that empathetic bond so near.

Fall

It crept in and set the world on fire,
The trees whispered its name with the wind,
And blushed with remembrance and longing.
It hasn't touched them all year,
But the trees don't forget.

It's sending the birds away south,
The bears hear it come and start foraging,
The bugs grow cold and dormant,
It hasn't touched them all year,
But the animals don't forget.

It is reddening the flesh of the apples,
And swelling the gourds to plentiful,
The sunflowers reach further for their light,
It hasn't touched them all year,
But the crops don't forget.

It is wrapping us in cozy blankets,
And filling our hands with warm mugs,
We draw in close to loved ones and share,
It hasn't touched them all year,
But the people don't forget.

Love Languages

I often think people have 2 sets of love
languages.
The ones we need spoken to us,
The ones we lived without too long and need,
Now more than ever.
And the ones we cannot help but speak,
The ones we were taught were
"Just what love looks like."

I need to be spoken to in words of affirmation,
I need to be spoken to in quality time.
After never feeling like enough,
And being neglected so often by so many,
Now more than ever,
I need to be reminded nearly constantly,
I am worth the time to be shown
"This is what love looks like."

I often can't help but speak in acts of service,
I often can't help but speak in gifts.
Everything I saw that people said was love,
Was back breaking emotional labor.
Now more than ever,
I'm trying to shift this viewpoint,

Trying to open my mind and keep asking,
"What does love look like?"

Things to Remember When it Gets Tough

How it feels to listen to a good song,
For the first time.
How it feels to know all the words,
To my favorite song.
How it felt to have them say I love you,
For the first time.
How it feels to hear them say I love you,
For the thousandth time.
How the earth and grass smell,
When it's just rained.
How the hot dry sand feels underfoot,
When it's been baked by the sun.
How it feels to be wrapped in a blanket,
Ready to drift off and dream.
How it feels to sip a hot cup of coffee,
With the whole day ahead of me.
How it feels to hold my purring cat,
He always knows when the day is tough.
How it feels to call my long distance love,

They're always willing to listen.
How it feels to cry at a good movie,
A genuine act of catharsis.
How it feels to laugh at a good joke,
A release of unbridled joy.
How it feels to lie in bed all cozy,
Sleep beckoning me.
How it feels to wake up in the morning,
Sunlight touching my face.

What Falling In Love Feels Like

When I was young it was,
A foreign sports car,
Just as fast and just as superficial.

As I grew up it was,
A game of five finger fillet,
Just as risky and just as thrilling.

When it came to my cat it was,
Microwave oatmeal,
Almost instant and just as easy.

When it was with my abuser,
It was a blind man in a construction site.
All red flags and caution tape I couldn't see.

After the abuse it was,
A brand new butterfly
Unsure after a great metamorphosis.

For the last time it was,
The cord for the parachute,

A safe landing after a fast fall.

When it is with myself,
It will be a tattoo,
Painful, a colorful scar, but permanent.

Falling in love never felt just one way,
It is a fingerprint.
Entirely unique every time.

Thank You, Rascal

Thank you for always being there for your
friends.
Thank you for setting boundaries with them.
Thank you for having open arms, an open heart
and mugs of tea.
Thank you for keeping the right people around
me.

Thank you for being true to yourself,
It's such a burden sometimes but I wouldn't trade
you for the world.
Thank you for being so strong so often,
Thank you for knowing when you can soften.

Thank you for creating a safe space for yourself,
Thank you for knowing what items bring
comfort and joy,
Thank you for always keeping snacks,
Thank you for keeping half-filled notebooks by
the stack.

Thank you for watching all the best shows,
Thank you for cooking all the best food,
Thank you for reading all the best books,
Thank you for doing all the best makeup looks.

Thank you for learning to love again after him,
Thank you for falling in love with the right
person, finally,
Thank you for trying to love yourself,
Thank you for sharing your love with everyone
else.

Thank you for collecting every cool stamp,
Thank you for collecting every letter, card, and
poem ever written for you,
Thank you for collecting super cool rocks,
Thank you for collecting adorable socks.

Thank you the most for every day you get out of
bed,
For trying so hard when things are tough,
Thank you the most for how hard you always
try,
To give yourself, me, a beautiful life.

Did You Know?

When our bones break,
They heal back stronger.
I choose to believe hearts do too,
The halves pulling together more solidly.

Pound for pound,
Those same bones are four times stronger than
concrete.
We were made for some heavy shit,
Don't be afraid to let me shoulder some of your
burden.

When struck by lightning,
Our skin holds the memory, a scar in that shape.
When falling in love these impressions are
made,
In the shape of their hands on our heart.

When we are in love,
Our brain release neurotransmitters that
resemble amphetamines.
Love really is our strongest drug.
Let's go through it's highs and lows together.

The naked human eye can distinguish,
Ten billion different colors,
Out of all of these my favorite is still,
The color you turn when I make you blush.

Each human has a wholly unique scent,
Let me get to know yours intimately,
By wrapping your arms around me,
Or having me between your sheets.

An adult human body is made from seven
octillion atoms,
While our universe holds only three hundred
billion stars.
We are not small by any means,
And I love you with every particle of my being.

We all have faint traces of gold in our blood,
So you are worth more than you think.
To me you are precious and priceless.
Don't waste a drop of your gold.

A Ring

I bought you a ring,
After we talked about it,
About how we'd spend our lives together,
About you coming to visit and going home,
Holding my promise of forever.

I bought you a ring,
And I knew where I would do it,
Where I'd take you beforehand too,
I wanted to give you the whole nine yards,
Asking down on one knee and all.

I bought you a ring,
And it's so beautiful,
It has frogs and your favorite colors,
I picked something so perfect for you,
And you'll never wear it.

I bought you a ring,
And I wear it every day,
It reminds me that I am foolish,
But it also reminds me that I am brave,
And capable of love despite my pain.

I bought you a ring,

You'll never even see,
But I'll look at it and think of you,
Of what it was like to love you,
And of what it was like to lose you.

I bought you a ring,
Because I thought you meant it,
Every time you promised forever.
And now I'm scared to try again,
To think another's promises are real.

I bought you a ring,
Because I really did mean it,
I wanted everything with you,
And I wish that feeling had left,
At the same time you did

I bought you a ring,
How many times?
How often have I mistakenly thought,
I would love someone forever?
But I bought *you* a ring.

Countdown

10. Something incredible is happening.
9. Our bodies have come together.
8. A beautiful tangle of limbs and love.
7. Gentle touches.
6. Not so gentle touches.
5. Thrusts and moans.
4. Bites and fingers and tongues.
3. Everything building up.
2. "I love you"s exchanged thousandfold
1. Ecstasy. Bliss. Euphoria.
0. Explosion.

My Light

My sunflower soul turns to face you,
My brightest light.
A new warmth fills my veins.
I swear you put the sun to shame.

I look at you like every star in the sky,
Lies under your skin.
A teary love fills my eyes.
I swear you'd glow in the dark.

You are every candle I ever lit,
To guide me through the night.
A sure direction fills my mind,
I swear you are my way home.

I feel like I am the moon with you,
I simply reflect your light,
A bright eclipse fills my view
I swear I could revolve around you.

The light breaking through yonder window,
Has always been you,
A timeless romance fills my heart,
I swear I am a Romeo and you a Juliette.

You are every point of light,
In a dark and scary world,
A new faith fills all of me,
I swear to always bask in you.

Trigger Warning

I told my doctor I felt like killing myself,
And he told me to stop smoking weed.
If I mention him by name in my note,
Would they take away his license?

My mom said I looked good,
Asked if I'd lost weight,
If I told her I never feel hungry,
Would she still see that as success?

My aunt passed away 3 months ago.
I don't know where the time went.
If she had been allowed to get better,
Would we have gotten along?

I don't belong in my body anymore,
I don't remember the last time I did.
If I get the surgery and grow a beard,
Would I feel at home in my skin?

I cry at least once almost every day,
I am so sad so often I can't hold it in,
If I gathered every fallen tear together,
Would there be enough to fill an ocean?

I am all made up of trauma and triggers,
I have a code I need to speak to be heard.
If I was held together by caution tape,
Would that be warning enough?

I Love You

Saying I love you feels like
Wrapping you in a soft blanket,
And my arms,
And holding you tight and close.

Saying I love you tastes like
Every kiss we'll ever share,
And every meal,
Cooked with all my affection.

Saying I love you sounds like
Every song playing on the radio,
And every poem,
And the way you made them all make sense.

Saying I love you smells like
Coffee brewed fresh in the morning,
And clean laundry,
And all the flowers in the world

Saying I love you looks like
You on the inside of the sidewalk,
As we hold hands,
Any small protection I can grant.

Between My Head
and Heart

Take it easy this time,
You can go slow,
Falling in love isn't a race,
You know?

Easy for you to say,
With all your logic,
Don't you know falling,
Is just like magic?

You can't fall under the spell,
So very easily,
Don't you bleed enough already,
Without offering yourself so eagerly?

I'd rather be bruised and broken,
As proof of my beating,
Than never feel this weightless,
Even if that part is fleeting.

Aren't you scared,
Of not making it through?

Scared of breaking so completely,
That you'll always be in two?

I will be in so many pieces,
By the time I'm done,
I'll be a beautiful mosaic,
Fragmented but reassembled as one.

If it truly is enough for you,
To live your life in love,
I suppose it doesn't matter what I say,
But it's hard looking on from above.

Your concern is touching,
And I'm sorry I've made it hard for you,
But love is what keeps me beating,
And pumping blood on through.

I Dream

I dream of Egypt,
And of Mars.
I dream of bees,
On my very own farm.

I dream of the ocean,
And exploring it's depths.
I dream of cleaning it,
Where the turtles are kept.

I dream of a restaurant,
Where I make the food,
And when everyone leaves,
They're in a good mood.

I dream of a wedding,
And right down the aisle,
Is my favorite person,
Who I've loved for a while.

I dream of three children,
Two boys and a girl.
I dream of raising them,
In a beautiful world.

I dream of a life,
So very well lived,
That when I am gone,
My memory's a gift.

Dearest Bea,

We have just met,
In one of my favorite Facebook groups,
A celebration of our queer community,
A place to be our truest selves.

This is where we found each other,
So maybe it won't surprise you,
Maybe a part of you always knew,
But I'm going to fall in love with you.

It's going to happen fast and hard,
I'm at the most vulnerable point in my life,
But I promise that's not why I do it.
It's not even at the top of the list.

At the very top of the list,
Is your incredible kindness,
In the face of all I have going on.
And your unwavering support.

Next on the list I have to say,
Is the way you can make me laugh,
When I've cried hard enough,
To make myself sick.

As if that weren't enough,
Your accent charms me infinitely,
Your eyes are the most beautiful,
And your smile makes the sun seem dim.

So maybe it won't be a surprise,
When I fall so irrevocably in love with you,
But I think it's incredible,
You'll fall in love with me too.

Apology to Myself

I'm so sorry for all the mean things I said,
While you were still healing,
I know it takes time,
And I should have been kinder.

I'm so sorry for how cold I've been to you,
While you needed someone to hold you,
You were so vulnerable,
And I should have treasured you.

I'm so sorry for loving the wrong people,
While you just needed me to love you,
But I didn't see you,
And I needed to look further.

I'm so sorry for the distance I put between us,
While you needed someone to be close to,
Some soft self care,
And I could have given you that.

I'm so sorry for the way I buried you,
While you needed room to breathe,
Something to look forward to,
And the kindness to uncover you.

I'm so sorry I haven't been patient with you,
While you've been finding yourself,
You were getting stronger,
And I should have appreciated that.

I'm so sorry for everything I cheated you out of,
While you were aching and longing for it,
Just because I was scared,
And I wasn't ready to be brave for you.

I'm so sorry for all the harm I caused you,
While you needed safety the most,
I was busy hurting you,
And I could have been protecting you.

I'm so sorry it took me so long,
While you were ready for it,
But I'm excited to know you again,
And I hope we can learn to love one another.

Cheers to All My Parts

To my bare face,
I have been trying to write you poetry,
Since the first day I covered you in makeup.

To my naked body,
I'm sorry I don't know how to look at you,
And see what my lovers do.

To my aching hands,
I know one day you'll no longer work,
But you've been brilliant partners.

To my beating heart,
Thank you for finding ways to mend yourself,
I know I don't make it easy.

To my anxious brain,
I promise we'll get to feel okay someday,
We'll just have to make it through this.

To my soulful eyes,
You hold so much in you, tears, longing, love,

I hope we never let go of the important parts.

To my fluid gender,
I know I barely understand you most days,
But I hope I'm living true to you.

To my thick thighs,
May you stay irresistible and biteable,
I am endlessly proud of you.

To my leonine spirit,
You are brave and breathtaking to no end,
I've never met anyone so fiercely loyal.

To my poet's mouth,
I hope you never stop speaking the metaphors
That made them fall in love with you.

To my wanderers feet,
May you one day find a place to plant
yourselves,
A place for your roots to flourish.

To every inch of me,
I want nothing more than to do you justice,
And repay you for your every kindness.